100 of the Most Beautiful Piano Solos Ever

ISBN 978-1-4768-1476-6

HAL•LEONARD®
CORPORATION

7777 W. BLUEMOUND RD. P.O. BOX 13819 MILWAUKEE, WI 53213

Visit Hal Leonard Online at
www.halleonard.com

AIR ON THE G STRING
from ORCHESTRAL SUITE NO. 3

By JOHANN SEBASTIAN BACH
1685–1750

ALWAYS

Words and Music by
IRVING BERLIN

Moderately slow

ALL THE THINGS YOU ARE
from VERY WARM FOR MAY

Lyrics by OSCAR HAMMERSTEIN II
Music by JEROME KERN

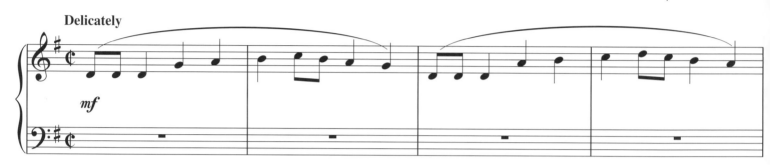

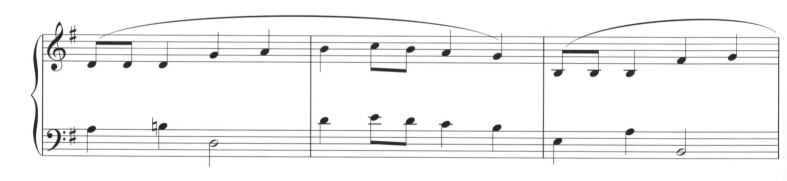

With expression

a tempo

Slower, freely

AND SO IT GOES

Words and Music by
BILLY JOEL

Slow Ballad, with rubato

BALCONY SCENE

from the Twentieth Century Fox Motion Picture WILLIAM SHAKESPEARE'S ROMEO AND JULIET

Words and Music by NELLEE HOOPER,
MARIUS DEVRIES, CRAIG ARMSTRONG,
TIM ATACK and DES'REE WEEKES

BALI HA'I
from SOUTH PACIFIC

Lyrics by OSCAR HAMMERSTEIN II
Music by RICHARD RODGERS

Andantino

Tempo I

BESS, YOU IS MY WOMAN

from PORGY AND BESS®

Music and Lyrics by GEORGE GERSHWIN,
DuBOSE and DOROTHY HEYWARD
and IRA GERSHWIN

Slowly

mp

With pedal

BALLADE POUR ADELINE

By PAUL DE SENNEVILLE

Slowly

BLACKBIRD

Words and Music by JOHN LENNON
and PAUL McCARTNEY

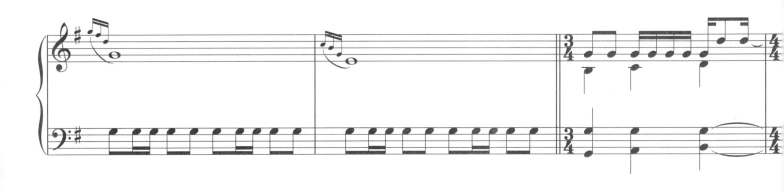

BRIDGE OVER TROUBLED WATER

Words and Music by
PAUL SIMON

BLUE MOON

Music by RICHARD RODGERS
Lyrics by LORENZ HART

Easy Swing (♫ = ♩♪³)

mf

CANON IN D MAJOR

By JOHANN PACHELBEL
1653–1706

Adagio

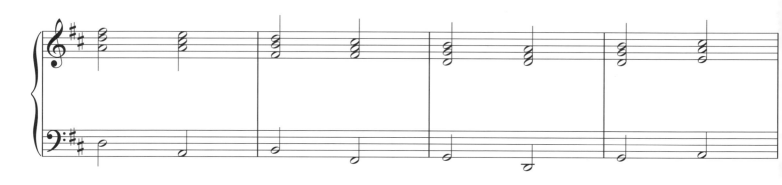

CHARADE
from CHARADE

By HENRY MANCINI

Moderate Waltz

With pedal

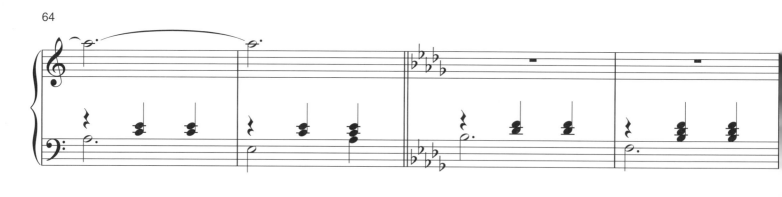

A CHILD IS BORN

By THAD JONES

Slow Waltz

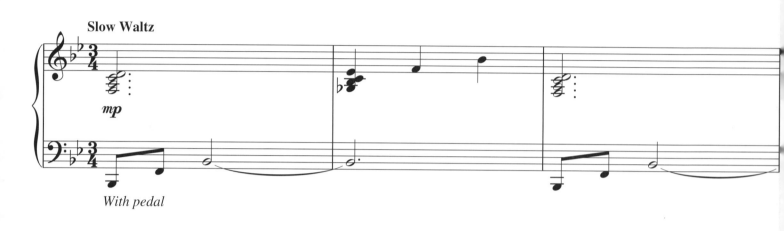

mp

With pedal

CLAIR DE LUNE
from SUITE BERGAMASQUE

By CLAUDE DEBUSSY
1862–1918

Andante très expressif

Calmato

Tempo I

DAYS OF WINE AND ROSES

from DAYS OF WINE AND ROSES

Lyrics by JOHNNY MERCER
Music by HENRY MANCINI

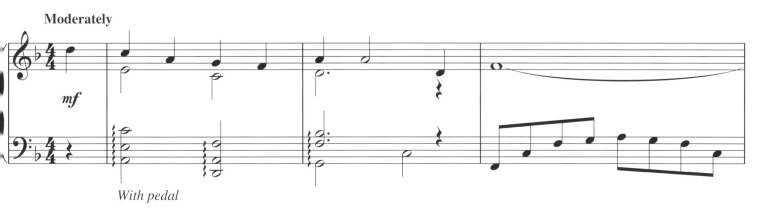

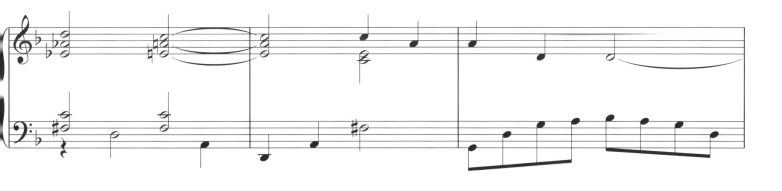

CRAZY WORLD
from VICTOR/VICTORIA

Lyrics by LESLIE BRICUSSE
Music by HENRY MANCINI

Moderately

mf

With pedal

DREAM

Words and Music by
JOHNNY MERCER

Slowly, with expression

With pedal

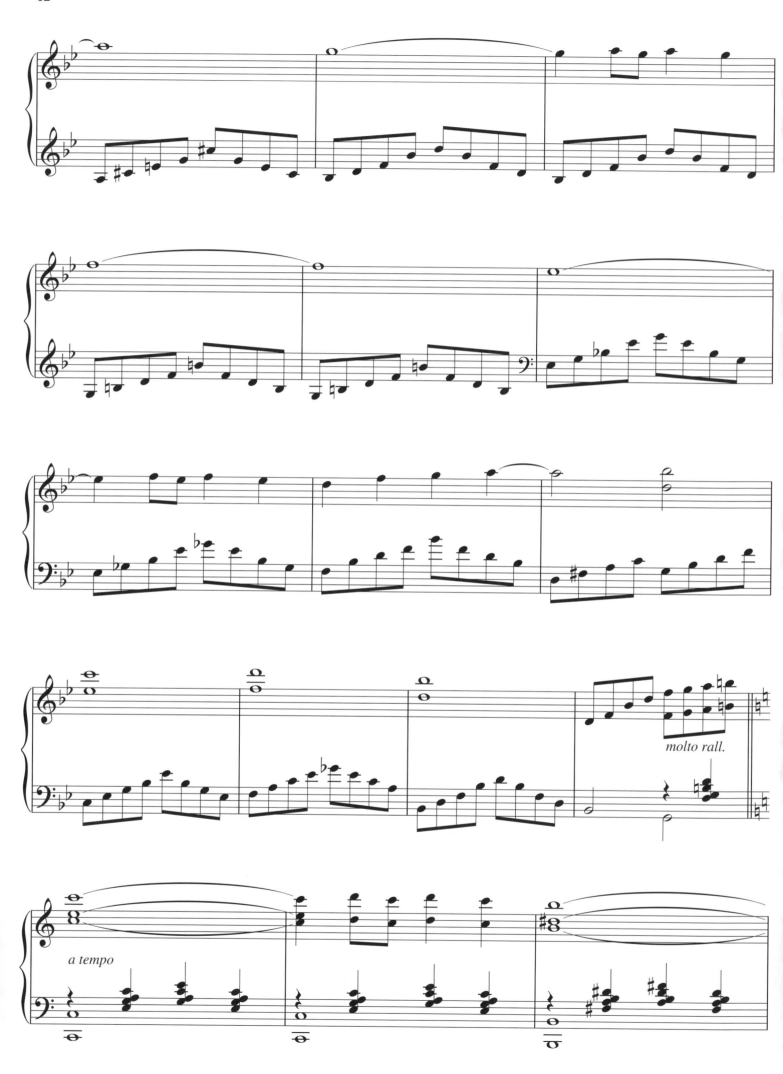

poco rall.

a tempo

EMILY

from the MGM Motion Picture THE AMERICANIZATION OF EMILY

Music by JOHNNY MANDEL
Words by JOHNNY MERCER

EMBRACEABLE YOU
from CRAZY FOR YOU

Music and Lyrics by GEORGE GERSHWIN
and IRA GERSHWIN

Whimsically

FIELDS OF GOLD

Music and Lyrics by
STING

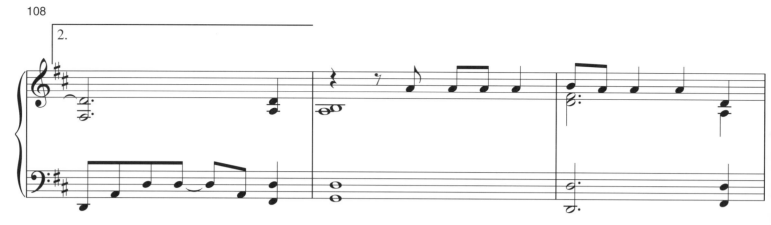

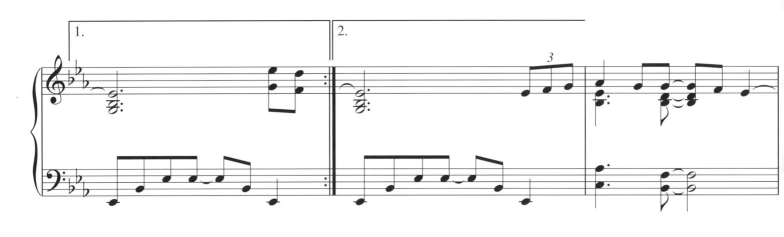

GOOD NIGHT

Words and Music by JOHN LENNON
and PAUL McCARTNEY

Slowly and tenderly

FRIENDLY PERSUASION

from the Motion Picture FRIENDLY PERSUASION

Words by PAUL FRANCIS WEBSTER
Music by DIMITRI TIOMKIN

FÜR ELISE
(Bagatelle)

By LUDWIG VAN BEETHOVEN
1770–1827
WoO 59

GENTLE RAIN
from the Motion Picture THE GENTLE RAIN

Music by LUIZ BONFA
Words by MATT DUBEY

Moderate Bossa Nova

HELLO

Words and Music by
LIONEL RICHIE

Slow Ballad

HELLO, YOUNG LOVERS
from THE KING AND I

Lyrics by OSCAR HAMMERSTEIN II
Music by RICHARD RODGERS

HI-LILI, HI-LO

Words by HELEN DEUTSCH
Music by BRONISLAU KAPER

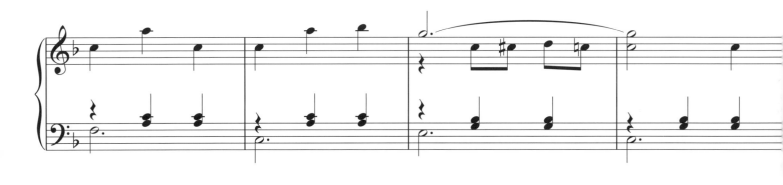

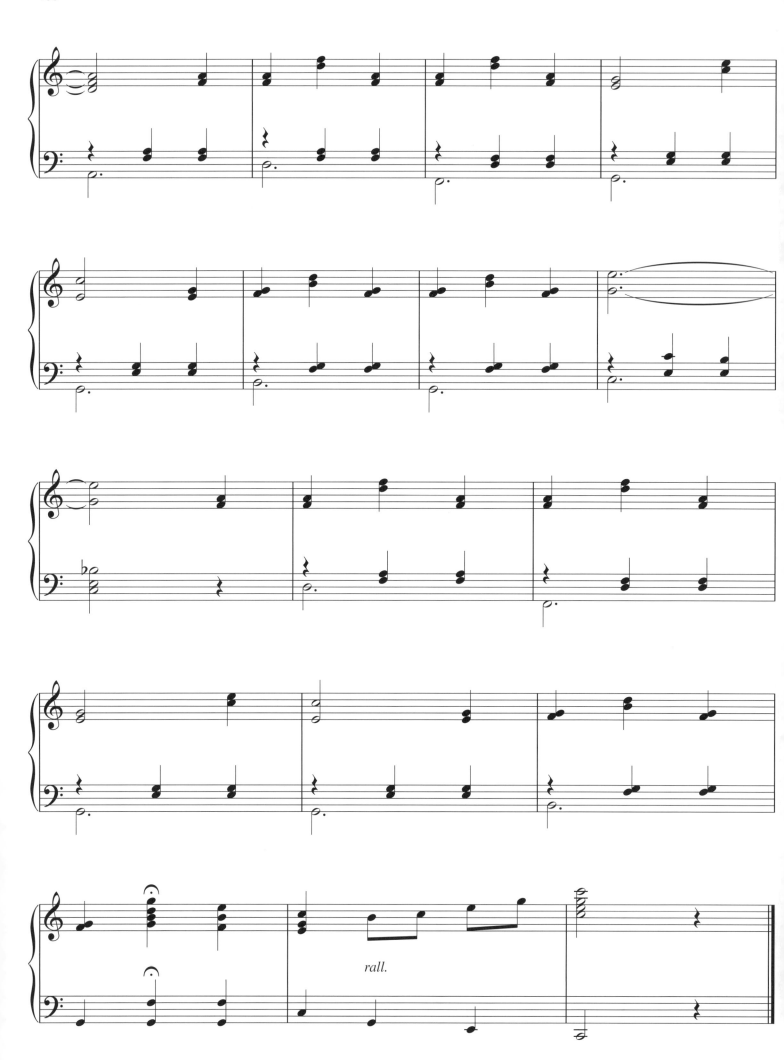

THE HIGH AND THE MIGHTY

from THE HIGH AND THE MIGHTY

Words by NED WASHINGTON
Music by DIMITRI TIOMKIN

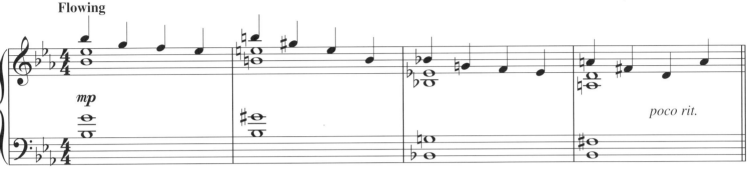

I DREAMED A DREAM
from LES MISÉRABLES

Music by CLAUDE-MICHEL SCHÖNBERG
Lyrics by ALAIN BOUBLIL, JEAN-MARC NATEL
and HERBERT KRETZMER

Moderately slow, with expression

146

I WILL ALWAYS LOVE YOU

Words and Music by
DOLLY PARTON

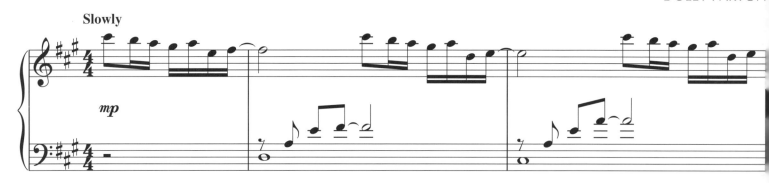

I'LL BE SEEING YOU

from RIGHT THIS WAY

Written by IRVING KAHAL
and SAMMY FAIN

I'LL STRING ALONG WITH YOU

Words by AL DUBIN
Music by HARRY WARREN

Moderately slow

With pedal

rit. e dim.

I'M IN THE MOOD FOR LOVE

from EVERY NIGHT AT EIGHT

Words and Music by JIMMY McHUGH
and DOROTHY FIELDS

CODA

IL POSTINO
(The Postman)
from IL POSTINO

Music by LUIS BACALOV

IMAGINE

Words and Music by
JOHN LENNON

Slowly and smoothly

IT MIGHT AS WELL BE SPRING
from STATE FAIR

Lyrics by OSCAR HAMMERSTEIN II
Music by RICHARD RODGERS

JEAN

Words and Music by
ROD McKUEN

Moderately

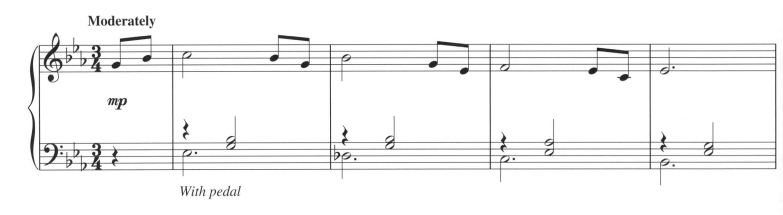

With pedal

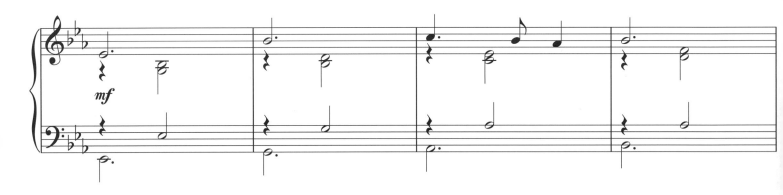

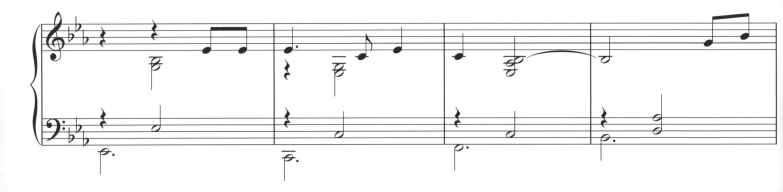

dim. e rit. al fine

p

LA VIE EN ROSE
(Take Me to Your Heart Again)

Original French Lyrics by EDITH PIAF
Music by LUIS GUGLIELMI
English Lyrics by MACK DAVID

LAST TANGO IN PARIS

By GATO BARBIERI

Moderate Latin

With pedal

LAURA

Lyric by JOHNNY MERCER
Music by DAVID RAKSIN

Slowly, expressively

LOVE IS BLUE
(L'amour est bleu)

English Lyric by BRIAN BLACKBURN
Original French Lyric by PIERRE COUR
Music by ANDRE POPP

LOVE IS HERE TO STAY

from GOLDWYN FOLLIES
from AN AMERICAN IN PARIS

Music and Lyrics by GEORGE GERSHWIN
and IRA GERSHWIN

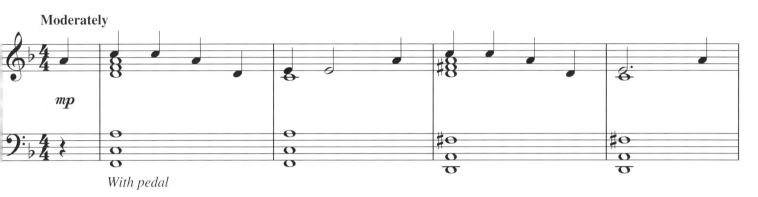

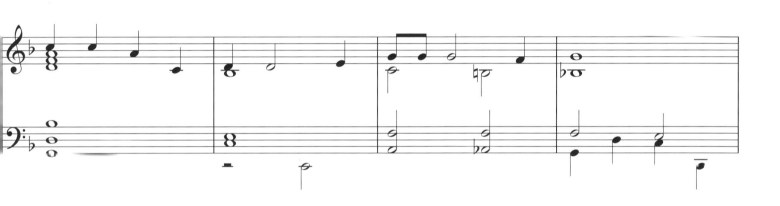

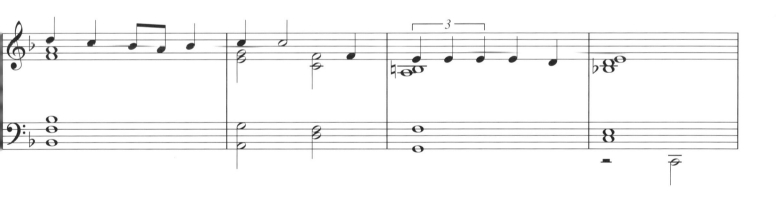

LULLABY OF BIRDLAND

Words by GEORGE DAVID WEISS
Music by GEORGE SHEARING

THE MAN THAT GOT AWAY
from the Motion Picture A STAR IS BORN

Lyric by IRA GERSHWIN
Music by HAROLD ARLEN

Slowly, freely

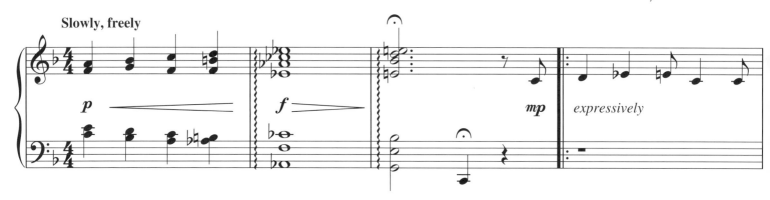

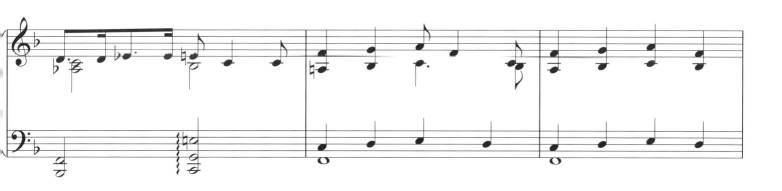

MEMORY
from CATS

Music by ANDREW LLOYD WEBBER
Text by TREVOR NUNN after T.S. ELIOT

Freely and expressively

MICHELLE

Words and Music by JOHN LENNON
and PAUL McCARTNEY

Freely

Moderately slow

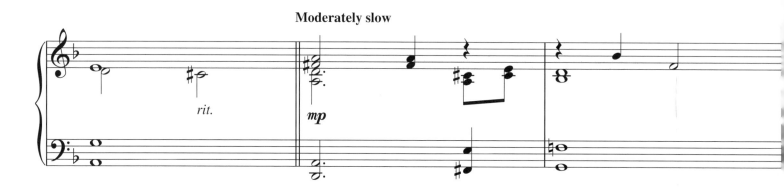

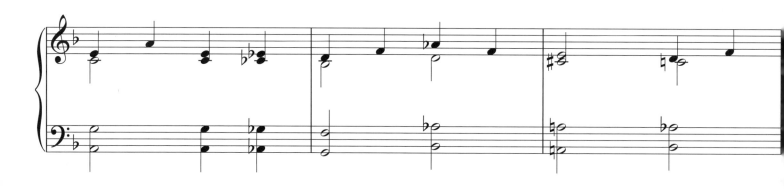

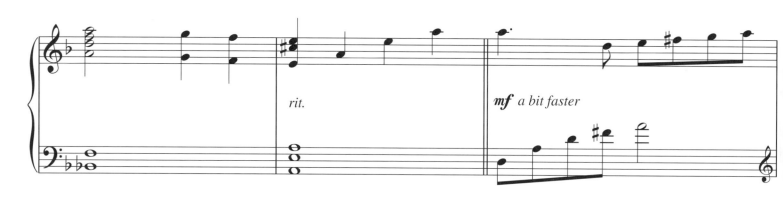

rit.

mf *a bit faster*

rit.

a tempo

3   3

MISTY

Music by ERROLL GARNER

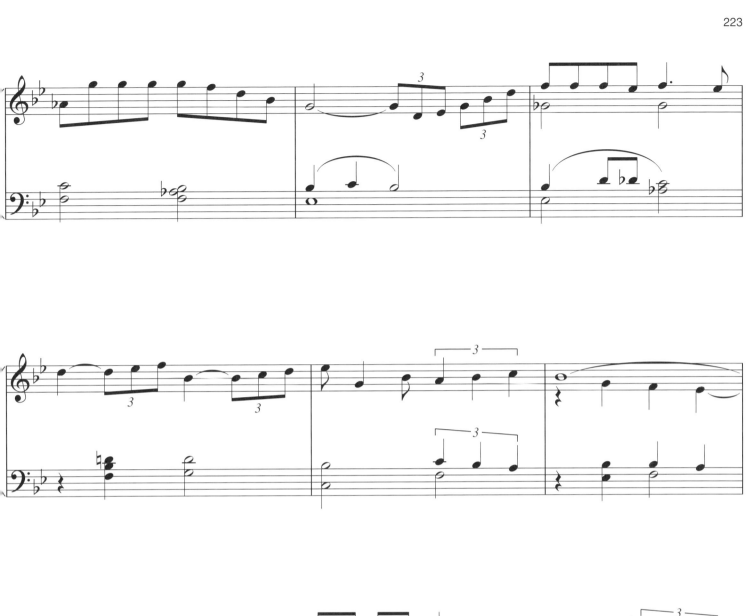

NIGHT AND DAY
from THE GAY DIVORCE

Words and Music by
COLE PORTER

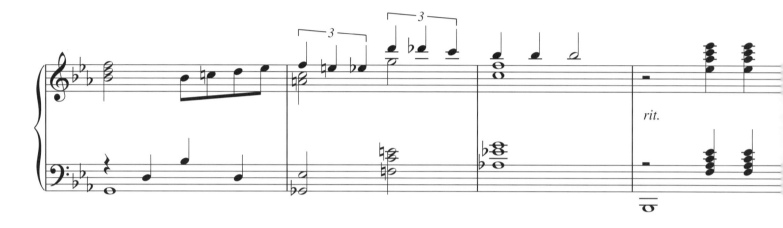

8vb

MOON RIVER

from the Paramount Picture BREAKFAST AT TIFFANY'S

Words by JOHNNY MERCER
Music by HENRY MANCINI

MOONLIGHT IN VERMONT

Words by JOHN BLACKBURN
Music by KARL SUESSDORF

With a steady beat

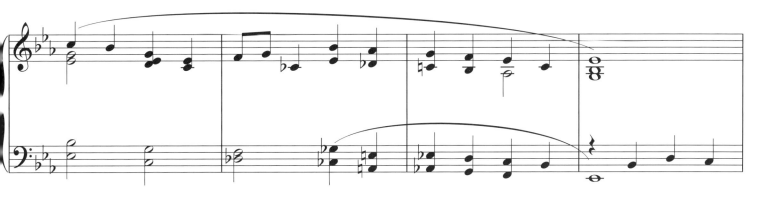

THE MORE I SEE YOU

from the Twentieth Century-Fox Technicolor Musical BILLY ROSE'S DIAMOND HORSESHOE

Words by MACK GORDON
Music by HARRY WARREN

Slowly, with feeling

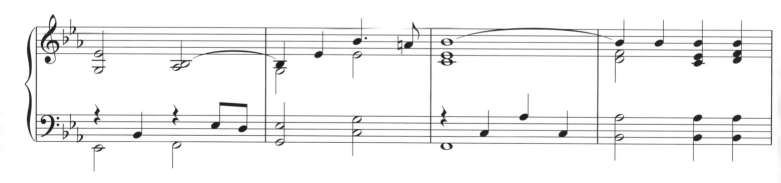

NADIA'S THEME
from THE YOUNG AND THE RESTLESS

By BARRY DeVORZON
and PERRY BOTKIN, JR.

ON MY OWN

from LES MISÉRABLES

Music by CLAUDE-MICHEL SCHÖNBERG
Lyrics by ALAIN BOUBLIL, JEAN-MARC NATEL
HERBERT KRETZMER, JOHN CAIRD
and TREVOR NUNN

Very slowly, but steadily

ON THE TRAIL
from GRAND CANYON SUITE

By FERDE GROFÉ

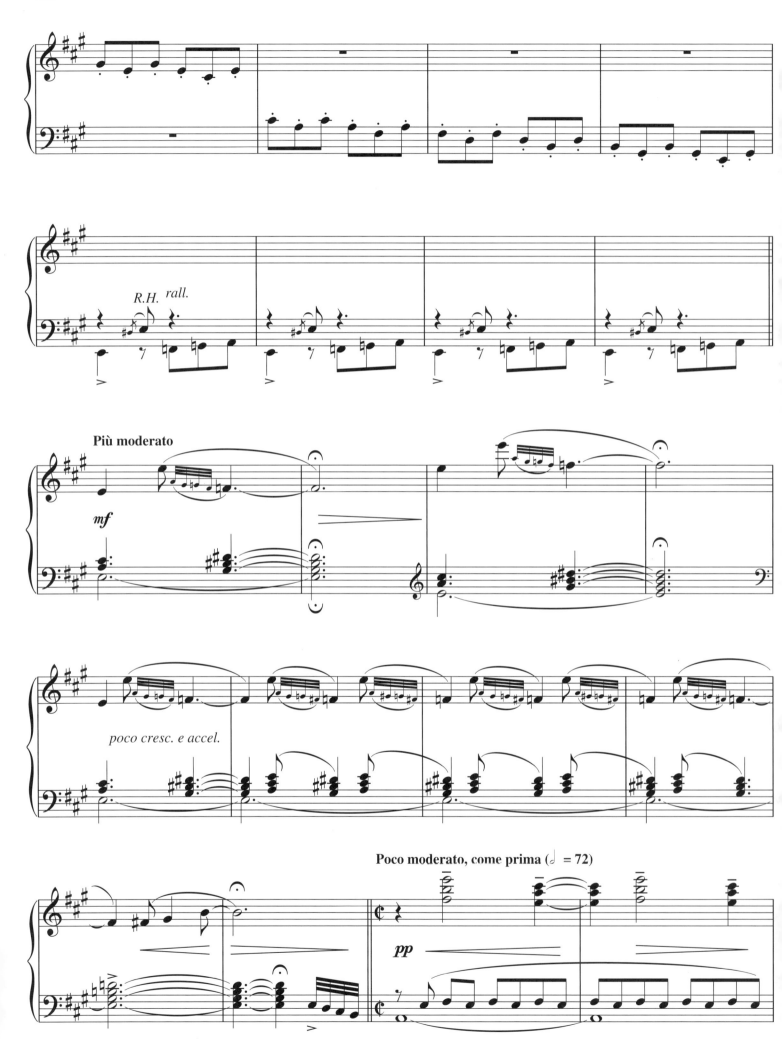

bring out the melody

dim. e rall. poco a poco

Meno mosso

mf

Allegro vivace (♩. = **132**)

ff

OVER THE RAINBOW
from THE WIZARD OF OZ

Music by HAROLD ARLEN
Lyric by E.Y. "YIP" HARBURG

ONCE UPON A TIME
from the Broadway Musical ALL AMERICAN

Lyric by LEE ADAMS
Music by CHARLES STROUSE

Somewhat freely, not too slow

OUR LOVE AFFAIR

Words and Music by ARTHUR FREED
and ROGER EDENS

Moderately, in 2

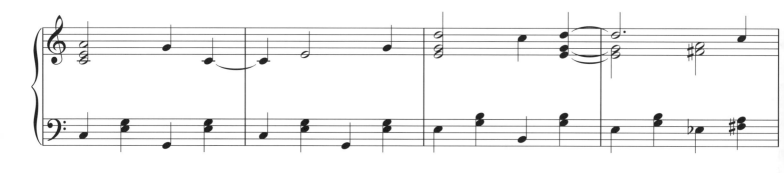

PIE JESU
from REQUIEM, Op. 48

By GABRIEL FAURÉ
1845–1924

PIECES OF DREAMS
(Little Boy Lost)
from the Motion Picture PIECES OF DREAMS

Lyrics by ALAN and MARILYN BERGMAN
Music by MICHEL LEGRAND

RIBBON IN THE SKY

Words and Music by
STEVIE WONDER

Slowly, wistfully

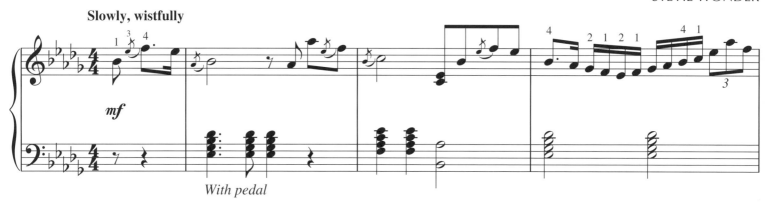

With pedal

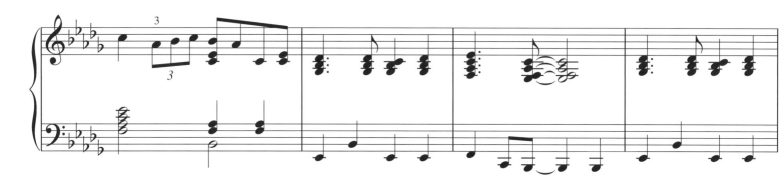

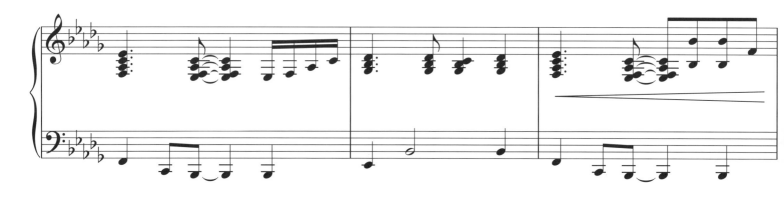

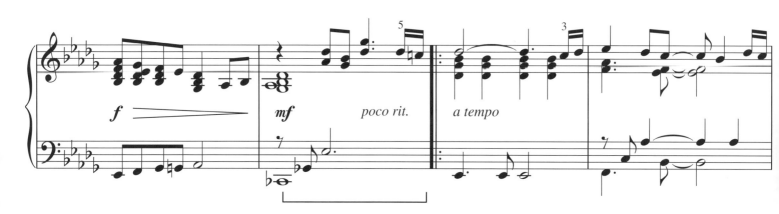

SECRET LOVE

Words by PAUL FRANCIS WEBSTER
Music by SAMMY FAIN

Moderately, with much tenderness

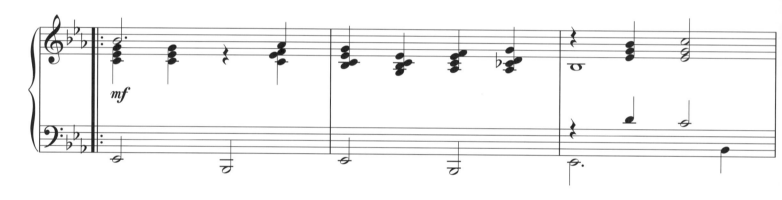

THE RIVER SEINE
(La Seine)

Words and Music by ALLAN ROBERTS
and ALAN HOLT
Original French Text by FLAVIEN MONOD
and GUY LaFARGE

'ROUND MIDNIGHT

Music by THELONIOUS MONK
and COOTIE WILLIAMS
Words by BERNIE HANIGHEN

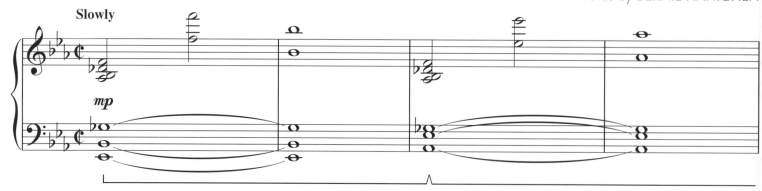

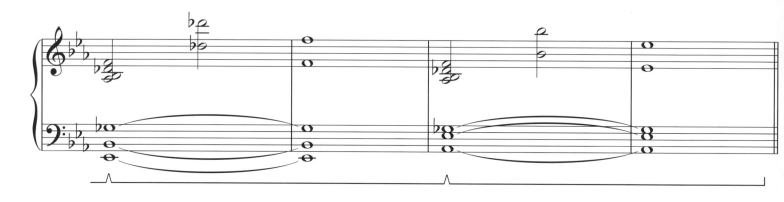

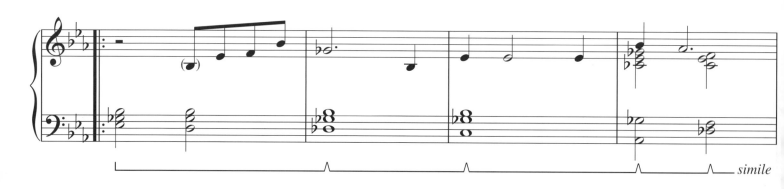

RUBY

Music by HEINZ ROEMHELD
Words by MITCHELL PARISH

Moderately

With pedal

THE SHADOW OF YOUR SMILE

Love Theme from THE SANDPIPER

Music by JOHNNY MANDEL
Words by PAUL FRANCIS WEBSTER

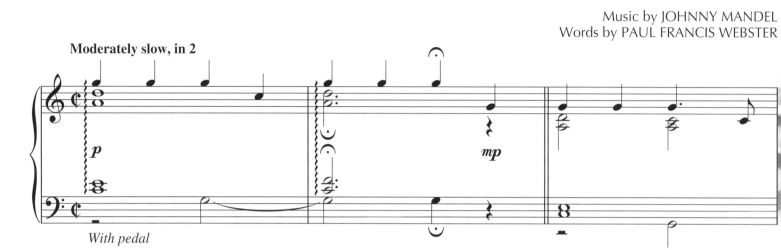

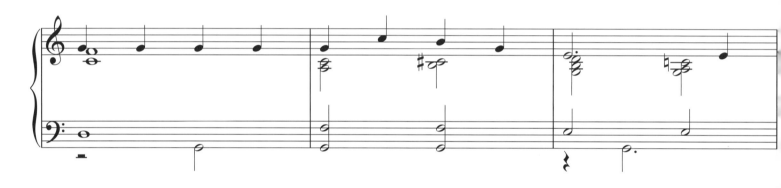

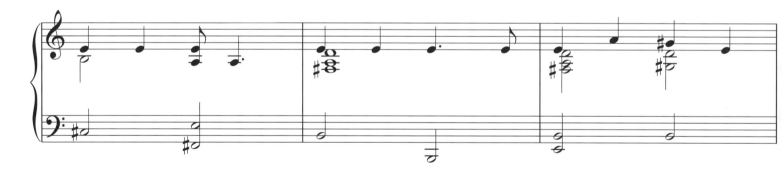

To Coda

D.S. al Coda

CODA

SKYLARK

Words by JOHNNY MERCER
Music by HOAGY CARMICHAEL

SMILE
from SMILE

Words by HOWARD ASHMAN
Music by MARVIN HAMLISCH

Soft-shoe Shuffle

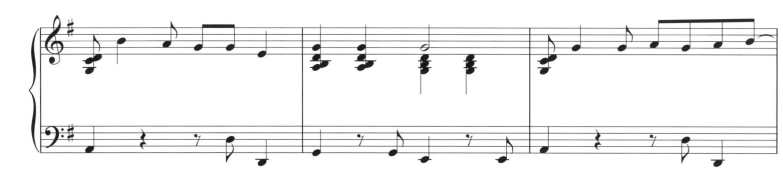

SOME ENCHANTED EVENING
from SOUTH PACIFIC

Lyrics by OSCAR HAMMERSTEIN II
Music by RICHARD RODGERS

SOME OTHER TIME
from ON THE TOWN

Lyrics by BETTY COMDEN and ADOLPH GREEN
Music by LEONARD BERNSTEIN

Freely, with sentiment

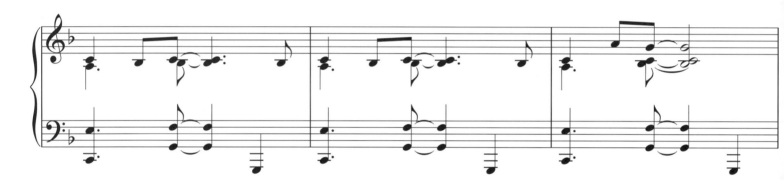

SOMEONE TO WATCH OVER ME

from OH, KAY!

Music and Lyrics by GEORGE GERSHWIN
and IRA GERSHWIN

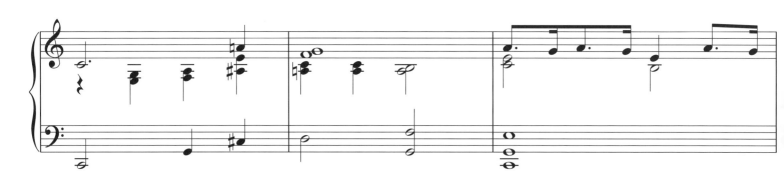

SOMEWHERE, MY LOVE
Lara's Theme from DOCTOR ZHIVAGO

Lyric by PAUL FRANCIS WEBSTER
Music by MAURICE JARRE

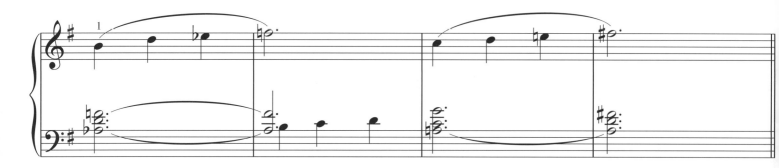

SPRING IS HERE

from I MARRIED AN ANGEL

Words by LORENZ HART
Music by RICHARD RODGERS

STARDUST

Music by HOAGY CARMICHAEL

Slowly and freely

STREET OF DREAMS

By SAM M. LEWIS
and VICTOR YOUNG

STORMY WEATHER
(Keeps Rainin' All the Time)
from COTTON CLUB PARADE OF 1933

Lyric by TED KOEHLER
Music by HAROLD ARLEN

With a double-time feeling

SUMMER ME, WINTER ME

Theme from PISCASSO SUMMER

Words by ALAN and MARILYN BERGMAN
Music by MICHEL LEGRAND

Moderately flowing, not too fast

SUMMERTIME

from PORGY AND BESS®

Music and Lyrics by GEORGE GERSHWIN,
DuBOSE and DOROTHY HEYWARD
and IRA GERSHWIN

SUNRISE, SUNSET
from the Musical FIDDLER ON THE ROOF

Words by SHELDON HARNICK
Music by JERRY BOCK

TARA'S THEME
(My Own True Love)
from GONE WITH THE WIND

By MAX STEINER

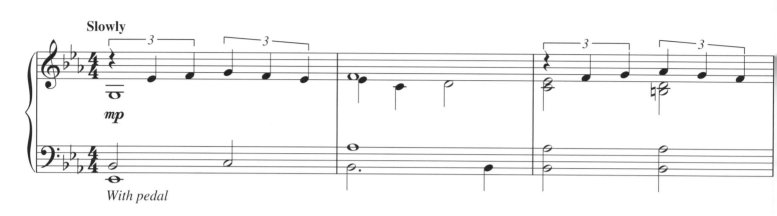

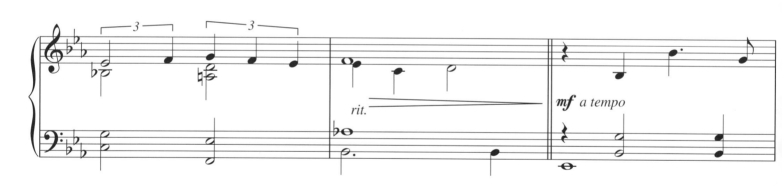

THAT'S ALL

Words and Music by BOB HAYMES
and ALAN E. BRANDT

Slowly, with expression

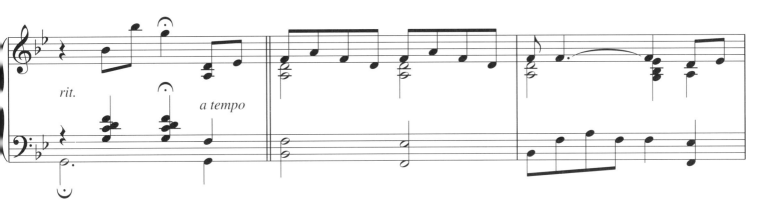

TENDERLY
from TORCH SONG

Lyric by JACK LAWRENCE
Music by WALTER GROSS

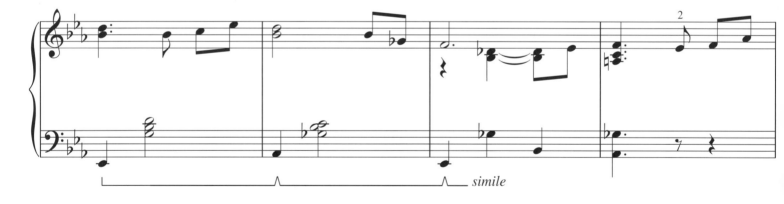

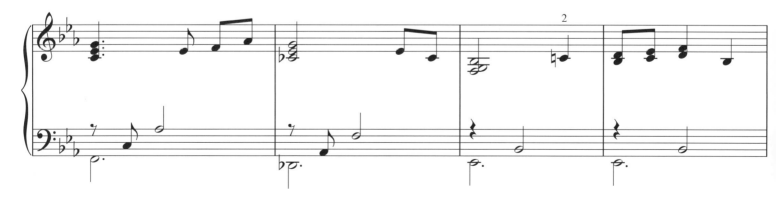

THE THORN BIRDS
(Main Theme)

By HENRY MANCINI

molto rit.

TILL THERE WAS YOU
from Meredith Willson's THE MUSIC MAN

By MEREDITH WILLSON

390

In the style of a Viennese waltz

TIME AFTER TIME

from the Metro-Goldwyn-Mayer Picture IT HAPPENED IN BROOKLYN

Words by SAMMY CAHN
Music by JULE STYNE

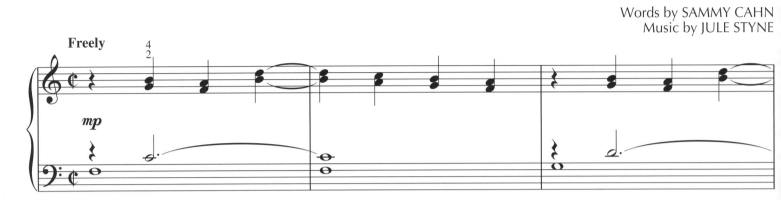

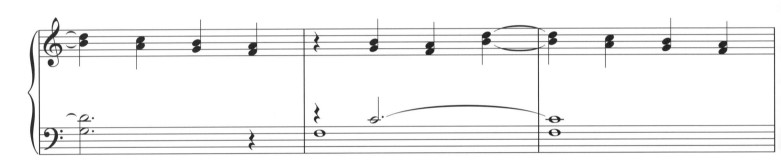

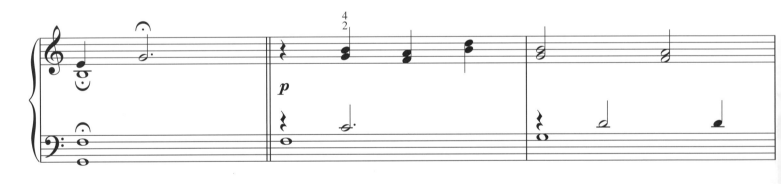

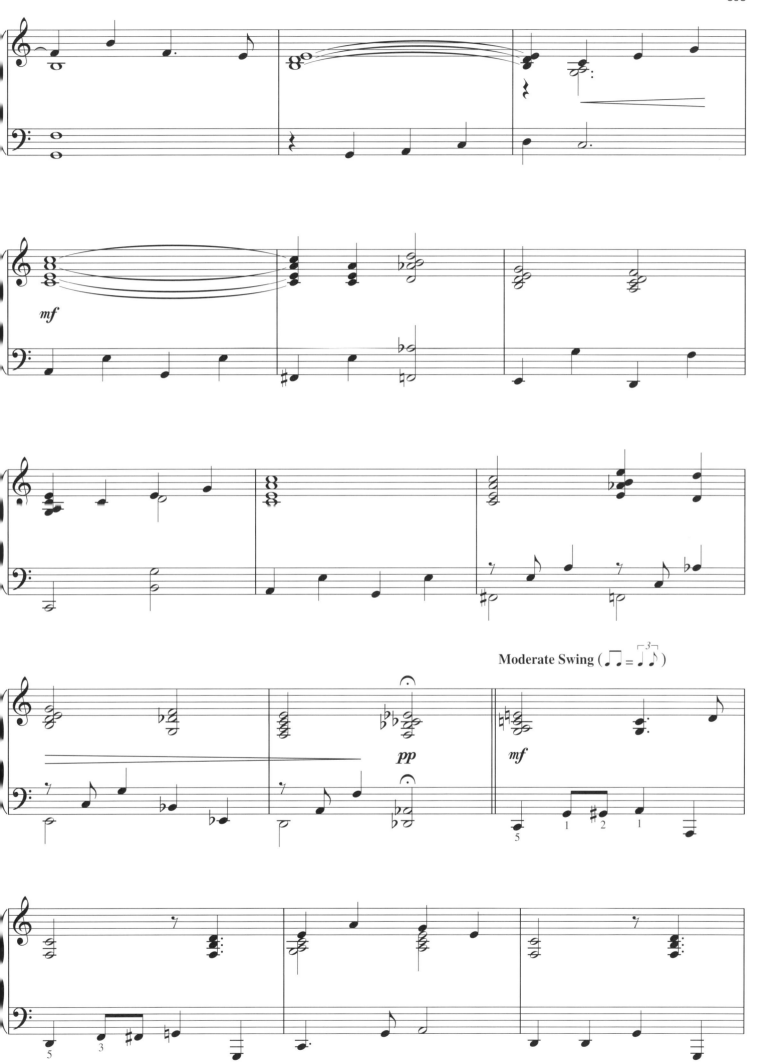

A TIME FOR LOVE
from AN AMERICAN DREAM

Music by JOHNNY MANDEL
Words by PAUL FRANCIS WEBSTER

Moderately slow

UNCHAINED MELODY
from the Motion Picture UNCHAINED

Lyric by HY ZARET
Music by ALEX NORTH

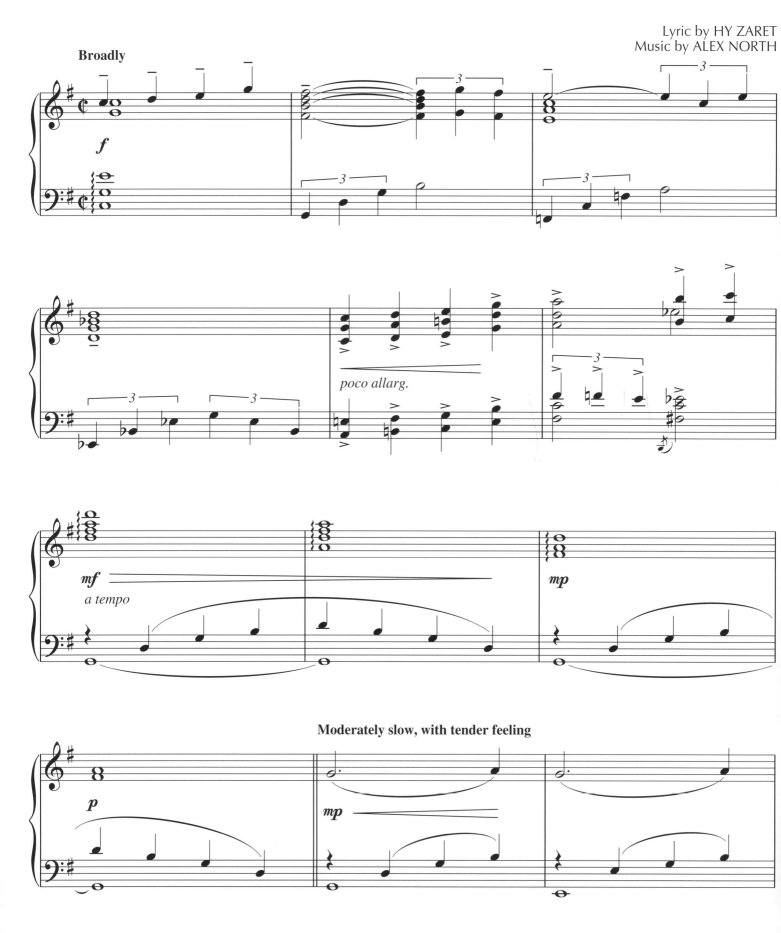

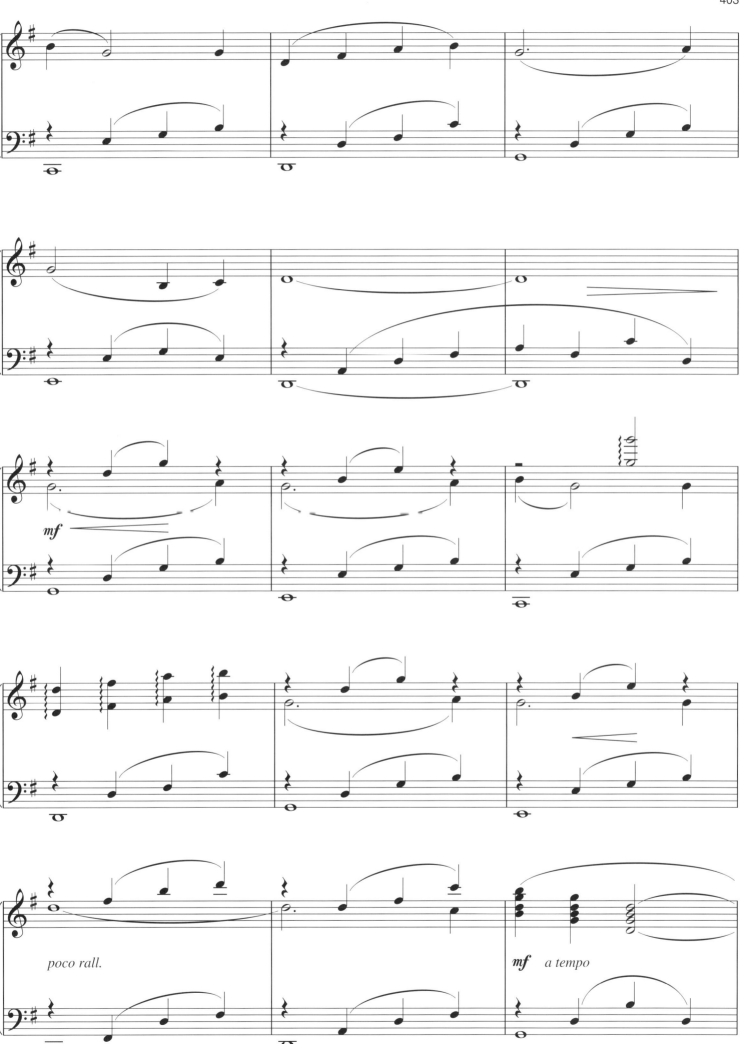

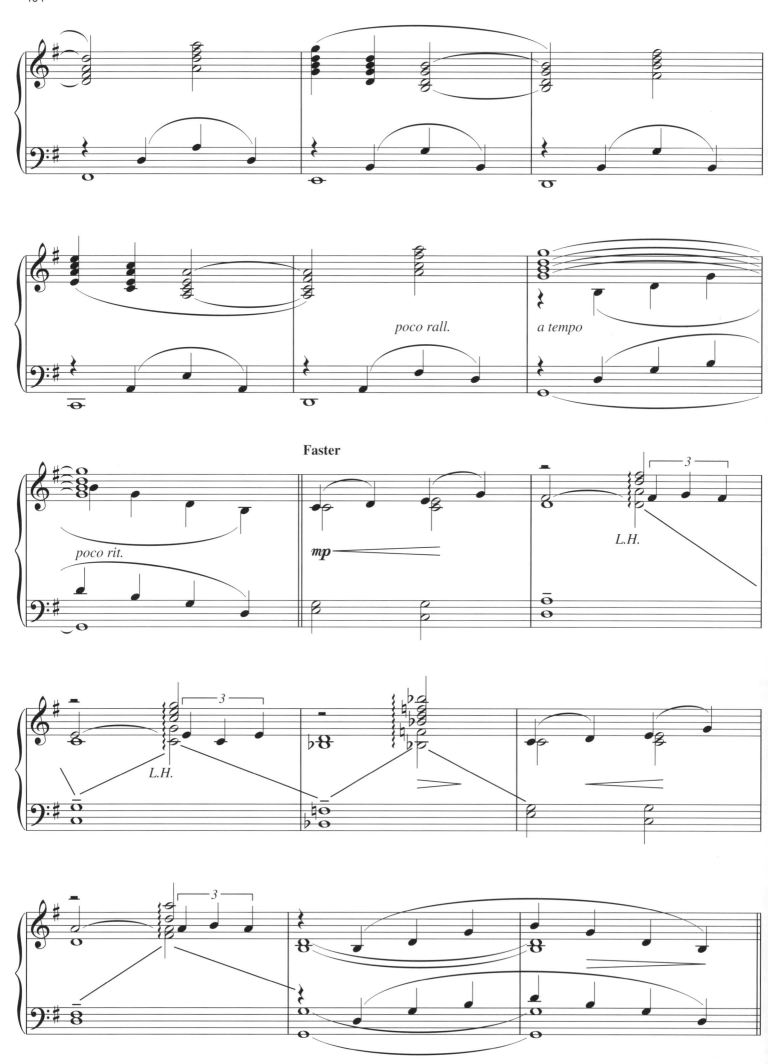

THE WAY YOU LOOK TONIGHT
from SWING TIME

Words by DOROTHY FIELDS
Music by JEROME KERN

Warmly, but with motion; Ballad style

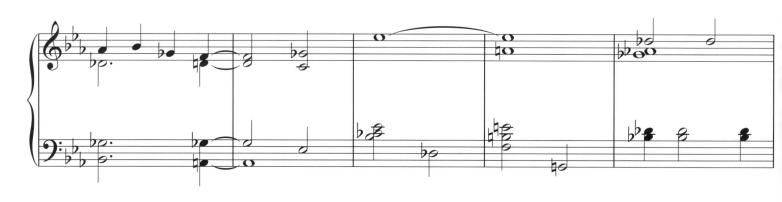

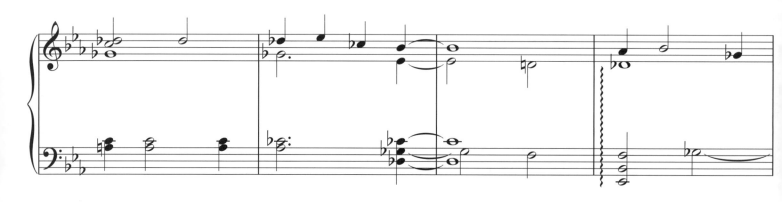

D.S. al Coda

CODA

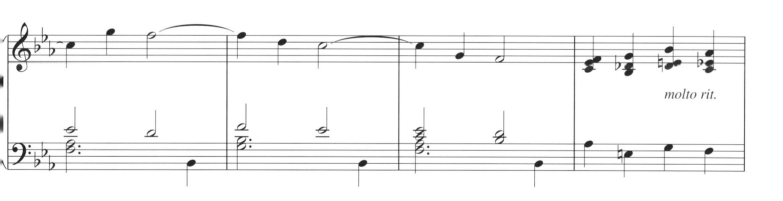

molto rit.

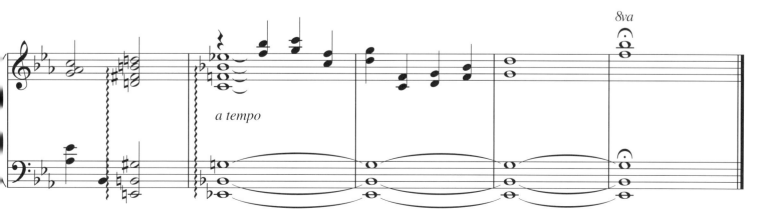

a tempo

8va

UNEXPECTED SONG
from SONG & DANCE

Music by ANDREW LLOYD WEBBER
Lyrics by DON BLACK

Slowly

With pedal

WE'VE ONLY JUST BEGUN

Words and Music by ROGER NICHOLS
and PAUL WILLIAMS

WHAT A WONDERFUL WORLD

Words and Music by GEORGE DAVID WEISS
and BOB THIELE

rall. e dim.

WHEN I FALL IN LOVE
from ONE MINUTE TO ZERO

Words by EDWARD HEYMAN
Music by VICTOR YOUNG

WHEN I GROW TOO OLD TO DREAM

Lyrics by OSCAR HAMMERSTEIN II
Music by SIGMUND ROMBERG

Moderate Waltz

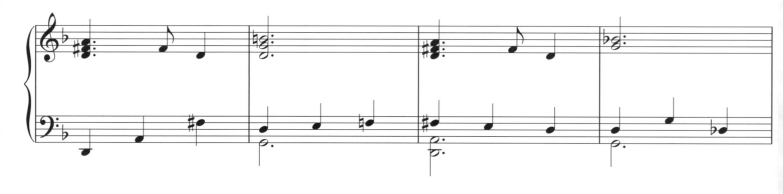

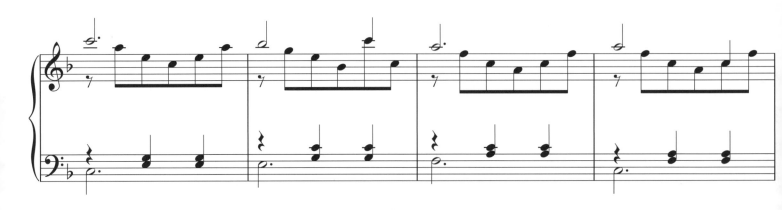

THE WHIFFENPOOF SONG
(Baa! Baa! Baa!)

Words by MEADE MINNINGERODE
and GEORGE S. POMEROY
Revision by RUDY VALLEE
Special Lyrics by MOSS HART
Music by TOD B. GALLOWAY

YOU LIGHT UP MY LIFE
from YOU LIGHT UP MY LIFE

Words and Music by
JOSEPH BROOKS

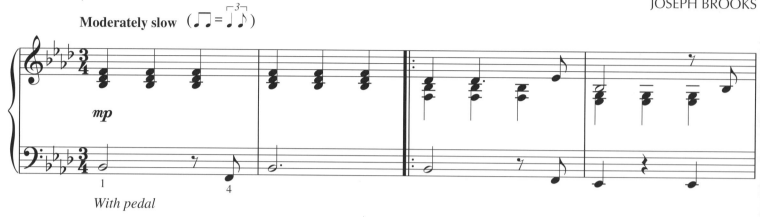

WISH ME A RAINBOW

Theme from the Paramount Picture THIS PROPERTY IS CONDEMNED

Words and Music by JAY LIVINGSTON
and RAY EVANS

Moderately slow

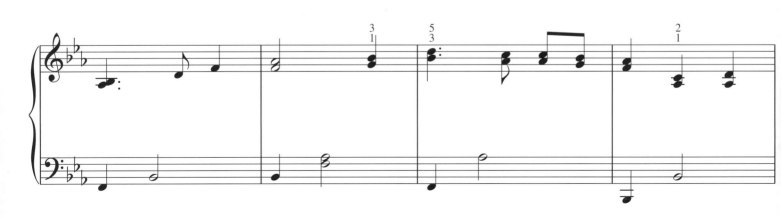

YESTERDAY

Words and Music by JOHN LENNON
and PAUL McCARTNEY

Moderately

YOU MUST BELIEVE IN SPRING

Lyrics by ALAN and MARILYN BERGMAN
Music by MICHEL LEGRAND

YOU RAISE ME UP

Words and Music by BRENDAN GRAHAM
and ROLF LOVLAND

YOUR SONG

Words and Music by ELTON JOHN
and BERNIE TAUPIN

Moderately slow, in 2

YOUR FAVORITE MUSIC
ARRANGED FOR PIANO SOLO

ADELE FOR PIANO SOLO – 2ND EDITION
This collection features 13 Adele favorites beautifully arranged for piano solo, including: Chasing Pavements • Hello • Rolling in the Deep • Set Fire to the Rain • Someone like You • Turning Tables • When We Were Young • and more.
00307585 ....$12.99

PRIDE & PREJUDICE
12 piano pieces from the 2006 Oscar-nominated film, including: Another Dance • Darcy's Letter • Georgiana • Leaving Netherfield • Liz on Top of the World • Meryton Townhall • The Secret Life of Daydreams • Stars and Butterflies • and more.
00313327 ....$17.99

BATTLESTAR GALACTICA
by Bear McCreary
For this special collection, McCreary himself has translated the acclaimed orchestral score into fantastic solo piano arrangements at the intermediate to advanced level. Includes 19 selections in all, and as a bonus, simplified versions of "Roslin and Adama" and "Wander My Friends." Contains a note from McCreary, as well as a biography.
00313530 ....$17.99

GEORGE GERSHWIN – RHAPSODY IN BLUE (ORIGINAL)
Alfred Publishing Co.
George Gershwin's own piano solo arrangement of his classic contemporary masterpiece for piano and orchestra. This masterful measure-for-measure two-hand adaptation of the complete modern concerto for piano and orchestra incorporates all orchestral parts and piano passages into two staves while retaining the clarity, sonority, and brilliance of the original.
00321589 ....$16.99

THE BEST JAZZ PIANO SOLOS EVER
Over 300 pages of beautiful classic jazz piano solos featuring standards in any jazz artist's repertoire. Includes: Afternoon in Paris • Giant Steps • Moonlight in Vermont • Moten Swing • A Night in Tunisia • Night Train • On Green Dolphin Street • Song for My Father • West Coast Blues • Yardbird Suite • and more.
00312079 ....$19.99

ROMANTIC FILM MUSIC
40 piano solo arrangements of beloved songs from the silver screen, including: Anyone at All • Come What May • Glory of Love • I See the Light • I Will Always Love You • Iris • It Had to Be You • Nobody Does It Better • She • Take My Breath Away (Love Theme) • A Thousand Years • Up Where We Belong • When You Love Someone • The Wind Beneath My Wings • and many more.
00122112 ....$17.99

CLASSICS WITH A TOUCH OF JAZZ
Arranged by Lee Evans
27 classical masterpieces arranged in a unique and accessible jazz style. Mr Evans also provides an audio recording of each piece. Titles include: Air from Suite No. 3 (Bach) • Barcarolle "June" (Tchaikovsky) • Pavane (Faure) • Piano Sonata No. 8 "Pathetique" (Beethoven) • Reverie (Debussy) • The Swan (Saint-Saens) • and more.
00151662 Book/Online Audio...........................$14.99

STAR WARS: THE FORCE AWAKENS
Music from the soundtrack to the seventh installment of the Star Wars® franchise by John Williams is presented in this songbook, complete with artwork from the film throughout the whole book, including eight pages in full color! Titles include: The Scavenger • Rey Meets BB-8 • Rey's Theme • That Girl with the Staff • Finn's Confession • The Starkiller • March of the Resistance • Torn Apart • and more.
00154451 ....$17.99

COLDPLAY FOR PIANO SOLO
Stellar solo arrangements of a dozen smash hits from Coldplay: Clocks • Fix You • In My Place • Lost! • Paradise • The Scientist • Speed of Sound • Trouble • Up in Flames • Viva La Vida • What If • Yellow.
00307637 ....$15.99

TAYLOR SWIFT FOR PIANO SOLO – 2ND EDITION
This updated second edition features 15 of Taylor's biggest hits from her self-titled first album all the way through her pop breakthrough album, *1989*. Includes: Back to December • Blank Space • Fifteen • I Knew You Were Trouble • Love Story • Mean • Mine • Picture to Burn • Shake It Off • Teardrops on My Guitar • 22 • We Are Never Ever Getting Back Together • White Horse • Wildest Dreams • You Belong with Me.
00307375 ....$16.99

DISNEY SONGS
12 Disney favorites in beautiful piano solo arrangements, including: Bella Notte (This Is the Night) • Can I Have This Dance • Feed the Birds • He's a Tramp • I'm Late • The Medallion Calls • Once Upon a Dream • A Spoonful of Sugar • That's How You Know • We're All in This Together • You Are the Music in Me • You'll Be in My Heart (Pop Version).
00313527 ....$14.99

UP
Music by Michael Giacchino
Piano solo arrangements of 13 pieces from Pixar's mammoth animated hit: Carl Goes Up • It's Just a House • Kevin Beak'n • Married Life • Memories Can Weigh You Down • The Nickel Tour • Paradise Found • The Small Mailman Returns • The Spirit of Adventure • Stuff We Did • We're in the Club Now • and more, plus a special section of full-color artwork from the film!
00313471 ....$16.99

GREAT THEMES FOR PIANO SOLO
Nearly 30 rich arrangements of popular themes from movies and TV shows, including: Bella's Lullaby • Chariots of Fire • Cinema Paradiso • The Godfather (Love Theme) • Hawaii Five-O Theme • Theme from "Jaws" • Theme from "Jurassic Park" • Linus and Lucy • The Pink Panther • Twilight Zone Main Title • and more.
00312102 ....$14.99

Prices, content, and availability subject to change without notice.
Disney Characters and Artwork TM & © 2018 Disney

HAL•LEONARD®
7777 W. Bluemound Rd. P.O. Box 13819 Milwaukee, WI 53213
www.halleonard.com

PLAY PIANO LIKE A PRO!

AMAZING PHRASING – KEYBOARD
50 Ways to Improve Your Improvisational Skills
by Debbie Denke

Amazing Phrasing is for any keyboard player interested in learning how to improvise and how to improve their creative phrasing. This method is divided into three parts: melody, harmony, and rhythm & style. The online audio contains 44 full-band demos for listening, as well as many play-along examples so you can practice improvising over various musical styles and progressions.
00842030 Book/Online Audio.............................. $16.99

BEBOP LICKS FOR PIANO
A Dictionary of Melodic Ideas for Improvisation
by Les Wise

Written for the musician who is interested in acquiring a firm foundation for playing jazz, this unique book/audio pack presents over 800 licks. By building up a vocabulary of these licks, players can connect them together in endless possibilities to form larger phrases and complete solos. The book includes piano notation, and the online audio contains helpful note-for-note demos of every lick.
00311854 Book/Online Audio.............................. $16.99

BOOGIE WOOGIE FOR BEGINNERS
by Frank Paparelli

A short easy method for learning to play boogie woogie, designed for the beginner and average pianist. Includes: exercises for developing left-hand bass • 25 popular boogie woogie bass patterns • arrangements of "Down the Road a Piece" and "Answer to the Prayer" by well-known pianists • a glossary of musical terms for dynamics, tempo and style.
00120517 .... $10.99

INTROS, ENDINGS & TURNAROUNDS FOR KEYBOARD
Essential Phrases for Swing, Latin, Jazz Waltz, and Blues Styles
by John Valerio

Learn the intros, endings and turnarounds that all of the pros know and use! This new keyboard instruction book by John Valerio covers swing styles, ballads, Latin tunes, jazz waltzes, blues, major and minor keys, vamps and pedal tones, and more.
00290525 .... $12.99

JAZZ PIANO TECHNIQUE
Exercises, Etudes & Ideas for Building Chops
by John Valerio

This one-of-a-kind book applies traditional technique exercises to specific jazz piano needs. Topics include: scales (major, minor, chromatic, pentatonic, etc.), arpeggios (triads, seventh chords, upper structures), finger independence exercises (static position, held notes, Hanon exercises), parallel interval scales and exercises (thirds, fourths, tritones, fifths, sixths, octaves), and more! The online audio includes 45 recorded examples.
00312059 Book/Online Audio.............................. $19.99

JAZZ PIANO VOICINGS
An Essential Resource for Aspiring Jazz Musicians
by Rob Mullins

The jazz idiom can often appear mysterious and difficult for musicians who were trained to play other types of music. Long-time performer and educator Rob Mullins helps players enter the jazz world by providing voicings that will help the player develop skills in the jazz genre and start sounding professional right away – without years of study! Includes a "Numeric Voicing Chart," chord indexes in all 12 keys, info about what range of the instrument you can play chords in, and a beginning approach to bass lines.
00310914 .... $19.99

OSCAR PETERSON – JAZZ EXERCISES, MINUETS, ETUDES & PIECES FOR PIANO
Legendary jazz pianist Oscar Peterson has long been devoted to the education of piano students. In this book he offers dozens of pieces designed to empower the student, whether novice or classically trained, with the technique needed to become an accomplished jazz pianist.
00311225 .... $14.99

PIANO AEROBICS
by Wayne Hawkins

Piano Aerobics is a set of exercises that introduces students to many popular styles of music, including jazz, salsa, swing, rock, blues, new age, gospel, stride, and bossa nova. In addition, there is a online audio with accompaniment tracks featuring professional musicians playing in those styles.
00311863 Book/Online Audio $19.99

PIANO FITNESS
A Complete Workout
by Mark Harrison

This book will give you a thorough technical workout, while having fun at the same time! The accompanying online audio allows you to play along with a rhythm section as you practice your scales, arpeggios, and chords in all keys. Instead of avoiding technique exercises because they seem too tedious or difficult, you'll look forward to playing them. Various voicings and rhythmic settings, which are extremely useful in a variety of pop and jazz styles, are also introduced.
00311995 Book/Online Audio.............................. $19.99

THE TOTAL KEYBOARD PLAYER
A Complete Guide to the Sounds, Styles & Sonic Spectrum
by Dave Adler

Do you play the keyboards in your sleep? Do you live for the feel of the keys beneath your fingers? If you answered in the affirmative, then read on, brave musical warrior! All you seek is here: the history, the tricks, the stops, the patches, the plays, the holds, the fingering, the dynamics, the exercises, the magic. Everything you always wanted to know about keyboards, all in one amazing key-centric compendium.
00311977 Book/CD Pack $19.99

HAL•LEONARD®
7777 W. BLUEMOUND RD. P.O. BOX 13819
MILWAUKEE, WISCONSIN 53213
www.halleonard.com

Prices, contents, and availability subject to change without notice.